Trail to the Spring

Trail to the Spring

poems by

Stacie Smith

SHANTI ARTS PUBLISHING
BRUNSWICK, MAINE

Trail to the Spring

Copyright © 2022 Stacie Smith

All Rights Reserved
No part of this document may be reproduced or transmitted in any form or by any means without prior written permission of the publisher, except in the case of brief quotations embodied in critical reviews.

Published by Shanti Arts Publishing
Designed by Shanti Arts Designs

Cover image by Tim Foster at unsplash.com

Excerpt by Zhenru from *Daughters of Emptiness*, Beata Grant, Wisdom Publications, 2003. Used with permission.

Shanti Arts LLC
193 Hillside Road
Brunswick, Maine 04011
shantiarts.com

Printed in the United States of America

ISBN: 978-1-956056-49-5 (softcover)

Library of Congress Control Number: 2022946945

for Rezi

ALSO BY STACIE SMITH

Open Burning

*Meanwhile the Earth:
Poems from Cougar Creek*

Real News

Second Sight
(a collaboration with June Campbell Rose)

Report from the Confluence

*If someone should ask me what this is
    all about,
Smiling, I'd point to the pure breeze
    and bright moon.*

~Zhenru

*The Universe has us surrounded,
    and we might as well surrender.*

~Swami Beyondananda

CONTENTS

THE SELF I THOUGHT

THE MAP ◆ 18
OUT OF THE BLUE ◆ 19
COQUILLE FALLS ◆ 20
PONDEROSA ◆ 21
MALA ◆ 22
THE BELL ◆ 23
ROSÉ ◆ 24
DRUG OF CHOICE ◆ 25
MIRAGE ◆ 26
WAITING TO BE SEEN ◆ 27
ABOUT TIME ◆ 28
BORROWED HOUSE ◆ 29
PROVENCE ◆ 30
THE SELF I THOUGHT ◆ 31
MY MIND THESE DAYS ◆ 32
MISCHIEF ◆ 33
THE CHICKADEES AND ME ◆ 34
SWITCHBACK TRAIL ◆ 35
FINAL QUARTER ◆ 36
GAME OF CHANCE ◆ 37

QUICKENING

GO BAG ◆ 40
APRIL 2021 ◆ 41
THE BIRTHING ◆ 42

FIRST SONG ◆ 43

DROP EVERYTHING ◆ 44

FOUR WALLS ◆ 45

HEAL-ALL ◆ 46

STILL ◆ 47

WILDFIRE SERIES I ◆ 48

WILDFIRE SERIES II ◆ 49

BLUE RIVER ◆ 50

TRAIL TO THE SPRING ◆ 51

BIRD COUNT, FEBRUARY 2021 ◆ 52

UP ALL NIGHT ◆ 53

QUICKENING ◆ 54

SLOW VIEW ◆ 55

MAYBE ◆ 56

CRISIS EVERYWHERE ◆ 57

PLAYA SERIES XII ◆ 58

PLAYA SERIES XIII ◆ 59

THIS PLACE

BLACKBERRIES ◆ 62

OCEAN PARK ◆ 63

EGRET ◆ 64

YAQUINA BAY ◆ 65

THIS PLACE ◆ 66

DUST ◆ 67

WHITE SPIDER ◆ 68

SPOTTED FAWN ◆ 69

MEMORIAL DAY 2021 ◆ 70

NOTHING HAPPENING ◆ 71

FINDINGS ◆ 72

CHICORY ◆ 73

NO TRAIL ◆ 74

WHO HEARS? ◆ 75

INTO THE ROOTS ◆ 76

NORTH BEAVER CREEK ◆ 77

SPOTTED HORSES ◆ 78

BOOK OF QUESTIONS ◆ 79

WAITING FOR RAIN ◆ 80

PINK IRIS ◆ 81

ACKNOWLEDGMENTS

The author expresses thanks to the editors of the following publications in which these poems first appeared:

Meanwhile the Earth: Poems from Cougar Creek: "On the Trail to the Spring"

Open Burning: "No Trail," "Coquille Falls," and "Mirage"

THE SELF I THOUGHT

THE MAP

In my dream, a map the size
and shape of a cottonwood leaf
showed me the way to your door.

I knocked, you opened.
You led me inside.
We sat by a glowing hearth.
You told me stories of your life
before the wars.

I told you stories of my life
before the drought, how
with help from strangers
I crossed deserts, then
sailed west.

In the silence between stories
we watched the fire, speechless,
amazed by whatever it was
that kept us alive until we met.

I showed you the map, a thin line
marking a trail that didn't exist
until I felt you call my name.

OUT OF THE BLUE
(DONNA'S PROMPTS SERIES XXIV)

out of the blue, pudding, rose, sweater,
*   sunrise, birthday*

Into the second year of the Plague
we were mad for distraction.
Some of us took up knitting—
sweaters and socks and tasseled hats—
others stayed in their kitchens, sunrise
to sunset, making puddings and pies
and birthday cakes from scratch.
A few planted gardens and tended
the roses in the village square.
Many found solace in books.
A certain child sought refuge in rhyme.
She sat by a window overlooking the surf.
Out of the blue, a poem came to her.
She picked up her silver pen.
She began to write:
"Into the second year of the Plague . . . "

COQUILLE FALLS

for Scout, Marie, and Judy

Into the seventh year of drought
I move not from a place of assertion
but down and down as if in a swoon.
I worry about the way a cloud looks.
Does it carry rain or fire?
The hills, my skin, the undergrowth
all dry as bones.

I follow my friends down a switchback trail.
They promise me a river still muscular and swift,
a sure remedy for this feeling of dying from thirst,
this falling as if being pulled toward a place
where my body knows more than anyone's mind.

Where the trail ends, the Coquille plunges down
taking my breath as it goes, flowing past stones
the size of small moons.
This is the place where the drought ends,
here where water meets stone head-on,
its force increased by its falling.

PONDEROSA

Mid-August now, the ground is parched.
The creek outside my door has dwindled
to a thread, but birds and two spotted fawns
still come to drink. Water is water to them,
no matter how shallow, diminished, or slow.

This summer the Ponderosa sheds needles
like dry rain, in response to the drought.
That pine is home to squirrels, and a place
for jays and crows and hawks to light and rest.
It offers up its shade, exudes its fragrance,
even as its vigor fades.

The human news is hideous these days
but even so, I'll try to emulate the pine—
share what's left of me, pay attention
to the beauty that remains. Rumi says
our tears improve the earth.
I'll offer mine, like rain.

MALA

Amber days flow by
like beads on a mala
being moved by the hand
of the one who prays.

Meanwhile a Stellar's Jay—
fierce dark and strong—
hunts branch and ground
for food for its young.

The mala revolves
as the mantra is spoken.
Fledglings when ready
fly the nest.

THE BELL

Out my south-facing window
a small bronze bell rings
in response to the breeze.
From this bell hangs
a narrow paper sail
filled with faded script
in a language unknown to me

It might say:
This is
the sound
of wind
in conversation
with bronze

It might say:
Whoever held
the brush
that wrote
these words
is gone

It might say:
Already
the wind
has forgotten
her name

ROSÉ

She lifts another glass
and suddenly forgets her name.
Nothing left to lose! She pours another,
offers up a wordless toast.

Outside her door the world
tilts toward oblivion.
She turns inside to look
for one redemptive clue.

She finds a breath, a pulse
and a surprising urge to pray.
But why? For what?
For who?

Another glass, and then a prayer
for rain—because the earth is dry.
And then for all us
who know not what we do.

DRUG OF CHOICE

While driving west I listen to an interview—
a woman who has written books about
addiction, getting sober in the process—
so I guess she knows whereof she speaks.

I hear her out while aiming for the coast
to score a little of my drug of choice—
the ocean's wild and bountiful enormity!

I've tried sobriety—it never lasts.
This craving for beauty always
gets the best of me.

MIRAGE

My mind's eye aims for
an oasis it believes it sees.
Thoughts form a caravan
of strange beasts burdened
with unearthly goods.

The promise of shade
and water and rest
pulls this caravan along,
the thought of no-thought
bringing up the rear.

Nothing but sand and sky.
Silence broken only by dry wind
and the tinkling of caravan bells.
Thirst has made a desert of my days.
Shall we meet at the well?

WAITING TO BE SEEN

Fearful of shadows cast
by what I think is real,
I fail to see the flame
that makes them dance.

Mistaking thought for truth,
my mind is easily beguiled
by patterns on the curtains,
not the windows they conceal.

Rumi told me this, and I agree.
I play hide and seek with stark reality,
afraid of being found, afraid of being
blinded by the glory waiting to be seen.

ABOUT TIME

It's about time sunlight poured
through these slatted blinds
while smoke from sweet incense
casts its moving shadow on the page.

It's about time my mind's eye opened
to the day precisely as it is, and looked
beyond its dread of what might be,

toward those jonquils in the vase,
this cup of tea, this book,
this candle flame, the actual,
the kind, the transparent air.

BORROWED HOUSE

with gratitude to Dawn

In a borrowed house
on the edge
of a quiet town
I sit each morning
learning to befriend
this silence,
unlearning the art
of the dodge.

Who am I
when old habits
begin to shift,
making room
for a new kind
of emptiness?

PROVENCE

I

My friends have gone
to the village.
I busy myself here
watching shadows
dance on my knee.

II

My mind is happy
having forgot
what is real
and what is not.

THE SELF I THOUGHT

The same way sugar melts in tea
is how I want to disappear
and feel my dissolution quicken
as it's stirred, and suddenly
the self I thought I was
is nowhere to be seen—
a crystal cup—
vessel
of transparency

MY MIND THESE DAYS

Energy
for argument
evaporates.
Ardent seeking
falls away.
Subject now
to subtle
condescension
by the young,
I've learned
to like what's
left of me and
it's not wrong if
I have nothing else
to say unless
it can be said
in song

MISCHIEF

These poems—who needs them?
They wouldn't even feed a snake.
They mean nothing to the deer.
The crow doesn't notice or care
what I put on this thin page.

But a feeling—something like mischief—
rises up in me, makes me want
to do this useless thing, makes me
want to see—and tell about—
the snake, the crow, the deer, the day.

THE CHICKADEES AND ME
(LOCKDOWN SERIES XIV)

Small birds come to the feeder
to peck at a suet cake,
the seeds embedded there.

I peck at the light embedded
in darkness, seeking clues.

The chickadees and me,
alike in our hunger,
doing what we need to do.

SWITCHBACK TRAIL
(COUGAR CREEK SERIES LXII)

All day long up and down
the switchback trail,
my body hauls my soul
lugging things it thinks it needs.

If not for a mirror on my wall
I wouldn't know I was so old—
but there it is: one harrowed
human face reflecting what it sees—

a world where war is legion, peace
a dream. I put down my load
and raise my battle flag—
white, for surrender.

FINAL QUARTER

I exist because my mother's bloods
were timed just so—that's as far
as I can go toward understanding
who—or why—I am.

In this final quarter of my life
attachments fade, ambition
slips away. Zeal subsides.
I have no argument, no plan,

no fear about whatever happens next.
I'm at the threshold of the great unload—
one foot in the here and now,
the other on the open road.

GAME OF CHANCE

Some lose it all and all at once—
wildfire, earthquake, hurricane—
some lose it slowly by attrition,
bit by tiny incremental bit.

I've lost a few things in my time—
my keys, my self, a friend or two,
a love, a hat, a shoe, a home,
a job, a cat, a game of chance.

I once lost hope but not for long—
it circled back around eventually
after a season of cold hard rain
followed by the freeze and then
the ice I skated away on.

QUICKENING

GO BAG
(END TIMES SERIES I)

Now the season of smoke begins
as the Bootleg Fire triples in size
not far east of here.

I want to just sit and write songs
of love and consolation, but all I can do
is face the day as it is, pray for rain
and be prepared to flee.

APRIL 2021
(COUGAR CREEK SERIES LIX)

Creek running low
underbrush tinder dry
nowhere left to go.
Even so
folks keep seeking
higher ground
reprieve from smoke
and bad news.
What's a body to do?
Dig in? Kick back?
Tune out? Tune in?
Dance on the head
of a pin?
Don't ask me!
I'm as lost
as anyone
my only guide
this ravenous
hunger for
staying alive.

THE BIRTHING
(END TIMES SERIES V)

A solitary crow, a sudden flash of indigo—
one more shard of beauty on this road trip
toward the setting sun.

Clear cuts mar the coast range slopes.
Scant remains of emerald forests—
parched and pale as far as the eye can see.

It looks to me as if the Earth is done
with this gestation; we've outgrown
the womb's largesse; it's done its job.

In utero, we didn't need to draw a breath.
Now here we are—the point of no return—
time to learn another way to breathe, or burn.

Home sweet home, it seems, has had enough—
eviction notice on its way—the birthing has begun.
Who will deliver us?

FIRST SONG

for Rezi (10/20/21)

One minute
drought
next minute
flood
in the instant
between extremes
a baby is born
gift from
another world
eyes bright
with bewilderment
first song
a necessary
cry
valiant
little warrior
shining with
new life
wielding
tiny fists
come to
disarm us

DROP EVERYTHING

Drop everything.
Something wants to be born.
For one undaunted moment
let the midwife that you are
take charge.

The world is fraught
with cruelty and fear but
something better wants to be.

No time to lose.
Move quickly now
toward the beautiful and right.
You know its name.
Let the midwife that you are
move us all a little toward the light.

FOUR WALLS

Dumb luck and bad angels
landed me here. I asked for it—
this life sentence, no parole,
these four grey walls.
Outside in the wider world
events that boggle the mind—
spawned by meanness and fear—
I didn't know how to help with any of it
so I broke a few rules. So what?

I robbed a bank of its false currency.
My imagination toppled monuments
to tyrants, lined up my enemies
against a wall and mowed them down
with a volley of hard kisses.
For these deeds I'm confined here,
with nothing but my escapee mind
to distract me, so I stay, dreaming
of a moon I can't see, remembering
the world's unspeakable beauty.

HEAL-ALL
(COUGAR CREEK SERIES LX)

In the garden Buddha's lap an apple
at his feet four sprigs of Heal-All
in an amber vase
one purple-blossomed offering
for each direction
one melting
one flooding
one burning
one where moon and sun come up
as the Earth keeps turning

STILL
(END TIMES SERIES II)

Here on the brink
the wind still blows.
The human storyline
still plays out.

Here on the edge
the sun still sets,
reddened now by smoke
from the Bootleg Fire.

Day still follows night.
Hunger still stalks
the hunter.

WILDFIRE SERIES I

A young doe rests in the shade.
A small bronze bell rings its single note
in response to a breeze. A crow flies
to a high branch.

Somewhere, someone thinks about
the good old days—where did they go?
Future collides with past
igniting this moment, now.

Somewhere someone prays for rain.
Elsewhere someone prays for wind.
On the other side of town someone
wonders how it feels to die.

A child reaches for the cookie jar.
A pretty woman dries a dish—
hovers on the brink of change—
tomorrow, wildfire.

WILDFIRE SERIES II

Before the fires began,
a sweet lassitude prevailed—
cool nights, warm dry days,
crickets trilling their familiar song,
gardens in decline yet bountiful.
Dear September, what have we done
to deserve you?

My forbears came west for reasons
I may never understand. I wonder—
were they lured by the myth
of new beginnings, running
from a shadowy past? Were they
hungry for gold? Room to move?
The thrill of the hunt?

Whatever pulled them here
to the far edge of this land—
it's in my blood and bones,
has held me in its thrall since
the day I was born, but now
there's no place left to go.
Flame surrounds us all.

Is there time enough for us
to find another, wiser, way to be?
The stars are there tonight
but shrouded by smoke
so I ask for guidance—
from a different kind of light—
toward repentance.

BLUE RIVER
(WILDFIRE SERIES III)

By the time we smelled smoke
it was already too late.

That's what they said
after the smoke had cleared
and there was nothing left
but ash and twisted steel
melted down to scrap.
Everything else, gone.
Meanwhile, a few miles east,
a Water Dipper—sturdy bird—
hops from stone to stone
then slips beneath the water,
disappears then pops back up,
hunting its way downstream.

Blue River—once a village,
now a ghost. A few evacuees
drift back to sift the rubble,
hunting for a trace of home.
Here and there, chimneys
made of river rock still stand.
Flowing west, the McKenzie carries
memory of ancient fir and cedar,
carries memory of creatures trapped
and swallowed by the blaze,
carries warning as it merges
with the sea.

TRAIL TO THE SPRING
COUGAR CREEK SERIES XXX

Clouds of sword fern pollen
backlit and golden fill the air.
Alder leaves drop
like bright rain.
Black fly buzz mingles with
sounds of the downhill stream.
Vine maple branches rattle
in young September's wind.

News of the world
doesn't enter this place
but I hear it anyway.
It's in my blood and bones
so it comes with me
on the trail to the spring.
It thirsts like I do
for the silence that sings.

BIRD COUNT, FEBRUARY 2021

Ice rain today, daphne in tight bud,
birds at the suet cake. A few of them
I recognize by sight and song:
Townsend's Warbler, Bushtit,
Black-capped Chickadee—some
I can't identify: dun-colored bundles
of feather and beak—they take a seed
and then they're gone.

Overnight, ice rain will turn to snow—
and now that I've begun to care about
the Warblers and the Chickadees
I want to understand the voice
that tells them when to come,
and where—and when—to go.

UP ALL NIGHT

If I could stay up all night
with rain on the roof,
new spring rain,
I would hear the soft thud
of flame burning logs
down to ember and ash.
And beneath this chair
the wood floor creaking
and under that
the sweet soil breathing
and then the granite,
the great heart
beating.

QUICKENING

It hasn't happened yet
but the forecast says it will.
No one knows exactly when
but you can feel it coming.
There's something rising up,
some kind of quickening,
a good hard storm.

Meanwhile there's nothing
to be done but wait and see
and hold on tight, and do
like the beach grass does
when a gale blows—
bend with the wind
and ride it out.
Hold on tight
to what sustains you.

SLOW VIEW

Easily amazed these days
I'm dazzled by the way
the winter sunlight
slides across the wall
and then illuminates
the cat asleep
on the window sill.

Outside my door it seems
a kind of frenzy reigns.
In light of this I'll ask
the long slow view to
join me for a cup of tea,
a cup of wine, a walk
along the Ridgeline Trail

and we'll discuss—or not—
the daily news and what
the pundits tell us it portends.
We're in the eye of some new
kind of hurricane, they say,
and there's no telling where
or when this story ends.

MAYBE

If your mind has become
a vessel of grievance
let the shock of daylight
shatter it.
Who knows? Maybe
the absence of wrath
helps miracles grow.
Maybe your tears
are a new kind of rain.
Maybe loss is gain.
Maybe your surrender
is victory's brightest flag.

CRISIS EVERYWHERE

To antidote the daily news
I listen to the rain or
to the hens next door or
to the wind or to my own
heart beating.

Headlines scream all day
for my attention:
!!!CRISIS EVERYWHERE!!!
I have to turn away at times
to keep on breathing.

I hope there's more than meets
the mortal eye—the human news
is getting old. I hope creation lets us
find our way to higher ground
before the trail goes cold.

PLAYA SERIES XII

An urgent sunrise woke me,
shouting color out across the lake.
Its imperative undid my sleep completely
so I got up—the only sane response
to daylight's unambiguous command
to rise and see and do and be.

But what? Do what? Be what?
I think we've done enough, been
witless agents of extinction long enough
and I begin to hear a different song.
It goes: *"We do not have to live
as if we are alone."*

> *Wendell Berry, "It All Turns on Affection,"*
> *Jefferson Lecture 2012*

PLAYA SERIES XIII

The news is bad
but the robin sings
as if it hadn't heard.
I want to be like that.

I'm not—but here's
what I would sing
if I knew how:
"Quick! Fall in love! Now!"

THIS PLACE

BLACKBERRIES

Fall Equinox 2021

On a trail to the beach, I see scat—
some other creature loves what I love—
blackberries—ripened in lee of the dunes,
bathed in sea mist, salty-sweet.

Yesterday they were blossoms
teeming with bees. Today they are
seed-bearing jewels filled with juice
the color of blood.

From flower to fruit—a season's
bountiful trajectory, and we are
equal beneficiaries—the bees,
the bears, and me.

OCEAN PARK
(SERIES II)

Amber grasses bend down,
casting shadows on the dune,
etching calligraphic lines
dictated by wind.

Below this dune, a cluster of gulls
all facing west, and beyond that
the Pacific surf, and beyond that
the vast blue highway for whales,
and then the horizon line so wide
and unbroken I can see
the earth's curve.

Shorebirds skitter and dart in unison
along the water's edge. All around me,
grasses write cryptic little poems
in the glistening sand.

EGRET
(COUGAR CREEK SERIES LXIII)

Knee deep in Beaver Creek marsh—
brilliant white, and poised to strike.

Meanwhile in the human slough
the plague seeks what it needs.

The egret spears its prey—one swift move.
I agree with what the earth must do.

YAQUINA BAY

Sun rises over the wetland.
Simple triumph—
night becoming day.

Two herons fly low
above the tidal stream.
The morning star fades.

A soul with hungry eyes
steps into the dawn
as if it were a prayer.

THIS PLACE
(COUGAR CREEK SERIES LII)

This place is not a person
but it breathes, it has a pulse.
The ground is animate,
and when I pay attention
I can see it shine.

Call me crazy, but I swear
this place has eyes.
I have a growing sense
they see through mine.
I can't explain—not yet—

but some new kind of knowing
beckons me. It has a voice,
and when I listen I can hear it
speaking from those mossy branches
of the broadleaf maple tree.

DUST

dust on the sill
spider in its web
rough road ahead
the pundits say—
but good news or bad
time sweeps us all
out the same door—
looks like the tide
of love's evolving
can't be turned

WHITE SPIDER

A white spider
rides the curled tip
of a calla lily
exquisite camouflage
white on white

she hides in plain sight
lures me close enough
to see her multiple eyes
her several delicate legs,
two of them outstretched
as if tasting the air.

How did she get here?
Did she ride a silk filament
at the mercy of the wind?

I step back slowly to view
her wider world; sword fern,
heal-all, equisetum, moss,
shadows cast by maple
and fir, creek running low
but steady, trickling its way
downhill.

SPOTTED FAWN

Across the creek in dappled light
a spotted fawn—bright-eyed, alert.
Through my window I watched
as it turned to its mother to nurse.

After a while the doe moved slowly
along the creek, fawn at her heels.
Then they vanished, slipping into
dark green shadow.

I remembered to breathe,
inhaling the marvel I'd seen,
exhaling wonder: the genius
of creation still at work
despite us.

MEMORIAL DAY 2021

What does the chickadee mean
when she chitters from the bush?
Is she signaling danger? Delight?
A motherlode of grubs or seed?

My mind wants explanations, always—
its hunger for meaning tires me out.
That's why I turn to the blank page
or to the ground or to a quiet friend.

Last day of May; we freshen flowers
on the graves of the fallen, we party,
take a day off work, congratulate
ourselves for outrunning the plague.

Meanwhile the reaper waits in the wings,
twiddling his thumbs, humming a tune—
sounds familiar—could be the wind
or a heart-beat, or the surf, or rain.

Rumi called it *"the nothing of roselight"*—
"the cold new air we breathe" when we die.
My mind's eye puts a flower on your grave—
I understand your leaving, but I can't explain.

NOTHING HAPPENING

May 2021

windchime ringing
dog barking
sparrow singing
petals falling
shadows dancing
heart beating
daisies shouting
pollen drifting
poppies blooming
grasses waving
fly buzzing
nothing
happening

FINDINGS

in memory of my father

I sit watching a honeybee
at work in the forget-me-nots.
She flies from bloom to bloom
stuffing her leg sacs with gold.
She'll carry her findings
back to the hive, unload,
then fly out again in search
of more blossoms to mine.

I admire the honeybee—
purposeful, tireless,
always on the move for
the good of the group.
I want to be like that—
but here I sit, immobilized,
dazed and amazed by
everything I see. What more
does the day want of me?

CHICORY

Eye to eye with chicory and hay
I see wild grasses wearing crowns
of radiant seed.
Cicadas drone from dry branches.
Stem-shapes of amber, platinum,
silver and gold form a lattice
where I suspend all thought.
Leaving contrivance beyond the gate
I will sit with these grasses
and wait for the moon.

NO TRAIL

*Owyhee Canyonlands,
May 2016*

sunlight shines
on the empty page
no sign at the trailhead
no trail no map no guide
only this moment
spawning this word
then the next.
what can be said
of this wilderness?
is there a way
to say "vast"
or "silent"
or "pure"
that rings true?
at times
to be lost
in the question
is the best
I can do.

~for Grace

WHO HEARS?
(COUGAR CREEK, SERIES XLVI)

A night bird with a single-noted call
signals from the ridge across the creek.
Who hears?

As darkness settles color fades.
Who sees?

The forest floor exudes sweet musk.
Who breathes it in?

Great Horned Owl swoops down
from high in the canopy.
Who escapes?

The creek flows downhill all night long
and into the next day's dawn.
Who remembers the night bird's song?

INTO THE ROOTS
(COUGAR CREEK SERIES LVII)

Inland a few miles from the sea, this steep-sided valley
embraces and holds the damp coastal air all night long,
transforming it into a heavy salt-scented mist.
Here, the call of the Hermit Thrush is muffled
as if sung through a veil of thick brocade.
Droplets form on broadleaf maple leaves
then fall to the forest floor like rain.

From a treehouse perch I watch it all—the mist,
the dark canopy, the beads of silver falling down
into the spawning stream or seeping into the roots
of alder, nettle, huckleberry, and fir.

Meanwhile, a plague is having its way with humankind.
In secret, I cheer it on, but don't tell a soul. I'd be burned
at the stake for speaking my mind. So here I stay,
on the fringe, where I pray for us all, without ceasing.

NORTH BEAVER CREEK
(COUGAR CREEK SERIES LXVIII)

A black bull plods through an emerald field,
his breath creating clouds that dissipate
behind him as he strides.

Low grey sky releases sudden rain.
Drops roll off the beast's glossy hide.
Where he steps, the ground shakes.

SPOTTED HORSES
(COUGAR CREEK SERIES XLI)

Spotted horses
cast their shadows
on the deep green field.

Sunset-colored Coho
move upstream
to spawn and die.

A madman
thinks he owns
the world.

A woman rises
with the dawn
to stir the soup.

My mind's eye searches
for a single
unifying clue.

Finding none,
it turns to you.

BOOK OF QUESTIONS

This day is a book of questions.
Turn the page—a sudden twist
of plot, a shift in point of view—
the hero dies, the city burns.
Maybe I'll skip ahead to the end,
jump over the hard part, where
foreboding creeps in, shadows
loom, there's only war and war,
too many grim contingencies.

Those crows who nest nearby
sound like they have answers—
they don't ask—they just proclaim.
I admire their certainty.

Always finish what you start—
I've tried to live that credo, tried
to persevere until a task is done
but now my eyes are weary—
my heart and mind are too—
so I'll put this book aside awhile
and listen to the crows for clues.

WAITING FOR RAIN

after a visit to Wickiup Reservoir

I'd give anything for rain—
enough to fill the reservoirs again.
Maybe some could fall on Lava Lake,
empty now of fish and fowl.

Maybe some could fall
above the timberline, where
if the air is cold enough
the rain will turn to snow—

and if we change our ways
and grow up fast—perhaps
this trip around the sun
won't be our last.

PINK IRIS

Cicadas foretell increasing heat.
Crows fly by, beaks open wide,
proclaiming thirst.

The worst is yet to come,
they say—
meanwhile we party.

Myself, I sit
in whatever shade I can find.
I pray, I laugh. I cry.

A pink iris too heavy for its stalk
leans down, its delicate blossoms
touching ground.

A bright yellow calla lily
stands tall, defying the odds,
shouting glory.

STACIE SMITH is a fourth-generation Oregonian. This is her sixth book of poems. She lives in her home town, Eugene, Oregon, in the Willamette River Valley.

Shanti Arts

Nature • Art • Spirit

Please visit us online
to browse our entire book catalog,
including poetry collections and fiction,
books on travel, nature, healing, art,
photography, and more.

Also take a look at our highly regarded art
and literary journal, *Still Point Arts Quarterly*,
which may be downloaded for free.

www.shantiarts.com

www.ingramcontent.com/pod-product-compliance
Lightning Source LLC
Chambersburg PA
CBHW022108040426
42451CB00007B/180